OUR AMAZING WORLD
SPIDERS

Kay de Silva

Aurora

Contents

Spiders	5		Spider Eggs	21
Anatomy	7		Spiderlings	22
Habitat	9		Black Widows	23
Senses	11		Brazilian Wandering Spiders	25
Spider Silk	13		Brown Recluse Spiders	27
Spider Webs	15		Crab Spiders	28
Venom	16		Diving Bell Spiders	29
Hunting	17		Jumping Spiders	31
Feeding	18		Tarantulas	33
Spider Colonies	19		Pest Control	34
Mating	20			

A beautiful Orb Weaver Spider in its web.

SPIDERS

Spiders belong to a group of animals called arthropods. Arthropods include arachnids, insects, and crustaceans (shrimp, crabs, lobsters, and barnacles). Spiders are not insects. Like ticks, mites, and scorpions, spiders are arachnids.

There are over 40,000 species of spiders found all over the world. They have been around for over 300 million years.

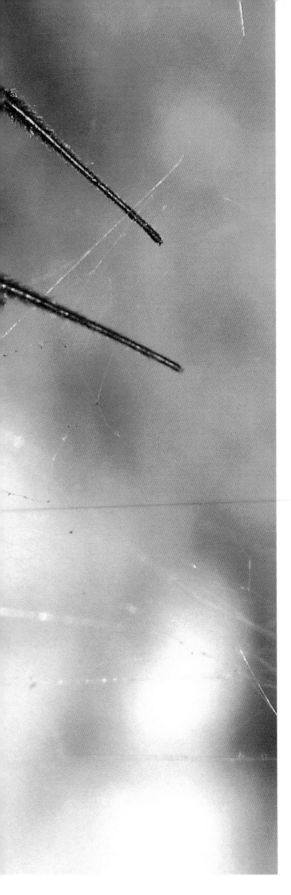

ANATOMY

Like all arthropods, spiders do not have skeletons or bones. Instead they have *exoskeletons*. This is a hard outer shell that covers and protects their bodies.

Arthropods also have segmented bodies and jointed legs. Spiders' bodies are made up of two segments or parts. The front part is called the *cephalothorax*. Their eyes, fangs, stomach, and brain are found here. Their legs are attached to this segment.

All spiders have eight legs and claws at the end of their legs. Each leg has six joints. So you could say that spiders have 48 knees!

The second part of spiders' bodies is their *abdomen*. The abdomen contains the heart, lungs, and digestive tract. It has six *spinnerets* or silk-producing glands that are located at the back end of the abdomen.

Notice the spider's jointed legs.

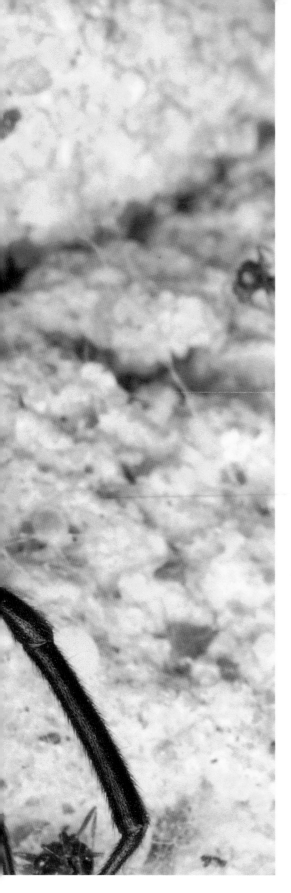

Habitat

Spiders are found anywhere insects can be found. This is because insects are spiders' favorite food. Spiders live all over the world, except in Antarctica.

Spiders also live in all sorts of places. Some live in trees and plants. Others prefer caves, rocks, and deserts. Spiders can even be found on the seashore. If you look carefully, you will find that they share your home, too.

A Black Widow in her lair.

SENSES

Most spiders have four pairs of eyes, but they have poor sight. They are mostly nearsighted, so they cannot see very far. The arrangement of spiders' eyes varies according to their type or *species*. What they can see depends on this arrangement.

Spiders are able to move their sets of eyes in different directions. This lets them scan what is going on around them. Unlike humans, who can tell which way is up even when our eyes are shut, spiders cannot. They rely on their sight for balance.

Spiders use their sense of touch to feel their surroundings and to detect movement and vibrations. They rely on these vibrations to alert them to danger or to be aware of food or *prey* that may be trapped in their webs. Spiders are hairy. These hairs are connected to nerves that give them information.

Spiders also have a strong sense of smell. Male spiders use this sense to help them find mates. Spiders also emit scents to mark their territory.

A close-up of a Wolf Spider.

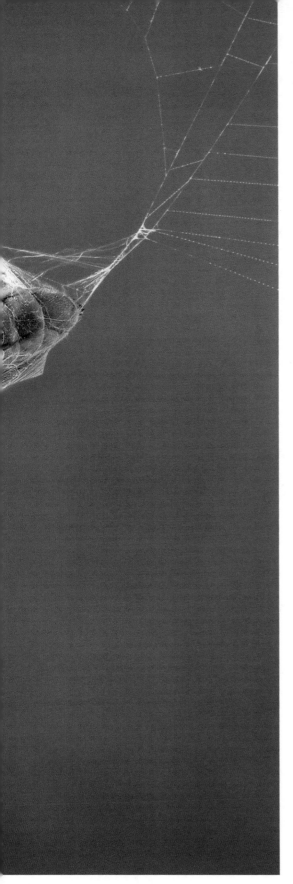

SPIDER SILK

Spiders squeeze a liquid from their *spinnerets* to make silk. This liquid is a protein that is thicker than water. The liquid hardens as it makes contact with the air.

Spiders can make sticky and dry silk. Spider silk is 30 times thinner than a human hair and very light, but do not let this fool you. It is the strongest fiber found in nature.

If you compare the same weight of spider silk and steel, silk is five times stronger. Spider Silk is also elastic, so it breaks only when stretched to two to four times its length.

Spider silk is used to weave webs, line nests, make egg sacs, and wrap cap-tured prey. Spiders also use their silk to help them travel. This is called *bal-looning*. To do this they fasten one end of a silk thread, called a *dragline*, to a sturdy place. Then they launch themselves into the air, letting the wind carry them to their destination, just like Spiderman!

An Argiope Spider wrapping a grasshopper in silk.

SPIDER WEBS

Spiders are born to spin; they do not need to be taught. A spider's web is its home. Some spiders use a web to catch their prey, while others prefer to hunt.

Spiders weave three types of webs. Orb-webs are the most common type. These are shaped like bicycle wheels. They can be very detailed and fancy. Spiders sit close to the center of the web lying in wait for their prey, which these sticky webs help them trap.

The sheet-web is the second type of web. Spiders weave a sticky web hori-zontally, like a sheet. They also weave non-sticky lines above it. These lines help knock its prey down, onto the sticky sheet below.

The third type of web is called the funnel-web. This web is wide at the top and tapers down gradually, just like a funnel. Spiders lie in wait for their prey, hiding at the bottom of the web.

Spiders eat their webs when they are no longer useful, so they are recycled to make new webs. Webs in use are correctly called spider webs. Abandoned webs are called *cobwebs*.

A spider creeping out of its funnel web.

A Green Lynx Spider with its fangs in a fly.

VENOM

Not all spiders have venom, but all spiders have fangs. Venomous spiders bite to catch prey when they are hungry. These spiders use their venom to paralyze their victims.

Other spiders' poisons are strong enough to kill their prey. The venom of some types or species of spiders such as the *Sydney Funnel Web* and the *Brazilian Wandering Spider* is the most dangerous to humans.

A Funnel Web Spider lying in wait to ambush its prey.

HUNTING

Spiders are *carnivores*, or meat eaters. Smaller spiders usually eat insects, but some of the larger ones also eat mice, bats, lizards, and small birds. Spiders are also *cannibals*, so they sometimes eat their own kind.

Only some spiders use webs to snare insects. Many spiders hunt their prey. Others sit camouflaged on plants or build burrows with trap doors and pounce on unsuspecting prey.

A Tarantula feeding on a frog in the Amazonian rainforest.

FEEDING

Hunting spiders have sharp fangs and fast-acting poison that they use to kill insects that are much larger than themselves. When spiders pierce their prey with their fangs, they squeeze out venom. The venom either paralyses or kills their victims.

Spiders cannot chew, so they have liquid meals. Venomous spiders use their poison to make the insides of their prey liquid. Web-spinners wrap their catch in a web and use their teeth to crush their prey's bodies. They then inject them with *digestive enzymes*, which turn their preys' insides into liquid. Then spiders simply suck up the insides of their prey.

A huge nest of a Social Spider colony in the Amazon, Brazil.

SPIDER COLONIES

Most spiders enjoy being alone. *Social Spiders*, however, are a species of spiders that form large groups or *colonies*. Some colonies have thousands of members. These colonies work together to build huge webs. All the spiders in the group share the prey that gets trapped in one giant web.

A male spider performing a mating dance.

MATING

Male spiders are smaller than females. Male spiders have to be careful to ensure that the females do not mistakenly eat them as they approach to mate. Some spiders have elaborate courtship rituals. Some will perform a dance, while others wrap up insects using spider silk to gift to the females.

A spider building an egg sac.

SPIDER EGGS

Spiders lay eggs on silken *beds*. They cover these eggs with silk *blankets*. Female spiders then wrap more silk around the eggs to make an *egg sac*. The sac is tough and difficult to rip apart. Spiders may produce several sacs. Each may contain up to several hundred eggs.

Spider mothers may stay with their eggs until they hatch. Others hide their sacs in their webs or under leaves. Spiders such as *Wolf Spiders* carry their sacs with them. When the babies hatch, they climb onto the mothers' backs until the first *molt*.

A Mother Wolf Spider waiting for her young to crawl onto her back.

SPIDERLINGS

Newborn spiders are called *hatchlings* or *spiderlings*. The hatchlings look much like adult spiders, except they are smaller. Sometimes their colors change as they grow older.

When spiderlings hatch, they usually stay in the sac until the first molt. Spiders molt by shedding their exoskeletons as they grow. Spiderlings will molt four to twelve times in their first year. After this they are considered adults.

A Black Widow carrying an egg sac full of hundreds of eggs.

BLACK WIDOWS

Female *Black Widows* are the most poisonous spiders in North America. These spiders get their name from the belief that females eat males after mating. Not all females eat their mates. They only do this if they accidently mistake the males for food.

Female Black Widows are easy to spot. They have a shiny black body with red markings. They also have a red hour glass pattern on the underside of their abdomens. Male Black Widows are brown or gray and have small red spots. Males are rarely seen, as they prefer to hide away.

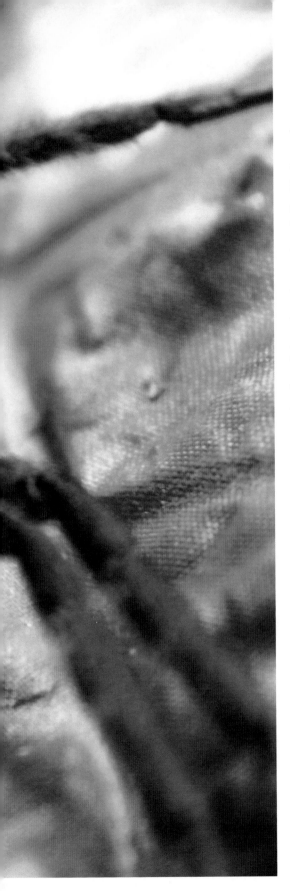

Brazilian Wandering Spiders

Brazilian Wandering Spiders are the second most deadly spiders known to man. They are commonly found in Brazil and the Amazon. These spiders have long legs that can grow up to four or five inches.

They are known as *wandering* spiders because they do not build webs. Instead, they are very active and love to explore the jungle floor. These spiders are *nocturnal*, which means that they prefer to hunt at night. During the day they like to hide in places such as rocks, plants, or termite mounds.

A deadly Brazilian Wandering Spider awaiting its prey.

BROWN RECLUSE SPIDERS

Brown Recluse Spiders are known as recluses because they like to hide in corners. They are light brown spiders and are recognized by the dark brown violin-shaped marking on their backs. These spiders are found in the United States, Canada, and many other parts of the world.

A Brown Recluse Spider camouflaged on dry winter grass.

A perfectly camouflaged Golden Crab Spider surprising a fly.

CRAB SPIDERS

There are over 2,000 species of *Crab Spiders* found all over the world. These spiders are *masters of disguise* because they *camouflage* their bodies to match their surroundings.

Their two front legs are longer than the rest, and they use these to capture their prey. They use their back legs to walk. These spiders get their name from the way they scuttle along sideways or backwards, just like crabs.

A Diving Bell Spider busy in its underwater home.

DIVING BELL SPIDERS

Diving Bell Spiders are the only spiders that live completely under water. They are found in ponds, lakes, and streams. They get their name from their webs, which they build on the surface of the water.

They then fill their webs with air bubbles from beneath. To do this they use the fine hairs on their abdomens to take bubbles from the surface of the water. These spiders then go under their webs whenever they need to breathe. They come up from time to time to fill their webs with air.

JUMPING SPIDERS

Jumping Spiders are found in tropical forests, mountains, and deserts. There are about 5,000 species of Jumping Spiders. These tiny spiders vary in color and have big eyes.

They are very good hunters and have better eyesight than most spiders. It is believed that they can see in color.

These spiders get their name from their ability to jump to over 40 times their height. They do not have strong leg muscles. Instead, they create pressure in their body fluid to propel them into the air. When they jump, they use a dragline in case they fall.

A playful Jumping Spider.

TARANTULAS

Tarantulas are large, very hairy spiders. There are about 700 species of Ta-rantulas. They are found in jungles and tropical forests of Africa, South and Central America, and the Southern part of North America.

Tarantulas do not live in webs. They prefer to live in underground burrows. They use their fangs to burrow, or they take over some other creature's burrow. Tree-dwelling tarantulas live in tunnels in trees. These spiders use their silk to make doors and line the walls of their burrows.

Tarantulas are nocturnal hunters that pounce on their prey. They usually eat grasshoppers, beetles, and other insects. The largest Tarantulas are called *Goliath Tarantulas* or *Goliath Bird-eaters*. These spiders are large enough to eat bats, snakes, hummingbirds, and fully grown mice.

Tarantulas use the hairs on their abdomen, which are like sharp barbs, to defend themselves. When they are threatened, they rub these hairs with their legs and shoot them at their predators.

A Greenbottle Blue Tarantula crawling on a branch.

A spider feeding on a Fruit Fly, the world's worst pest.

PEST CONTROL

Many people fear spiders. However, most spider species are harmless. Those that are venomous bite humans only when they feel that they are in danger.

Spiders are known as friends of humankind because they keep the insect population under control. Spiders eat more insects than birds and bats taken together. In this way, spiders help farmers to control pests that destroy crops.

Next time you see a spider, take some time to quietly observe it. Spiders are attractive, fascinating creatures that make our world a better place.

OUR AMAZING WORLD

COLLECT THEM ALL

WWW.OURAMAZINGWORLDBOOKS.COM

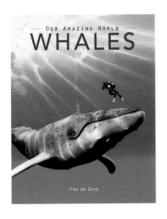

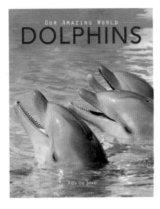

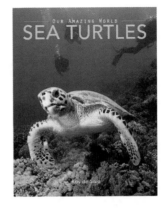

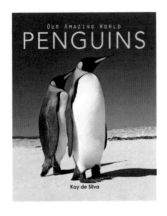

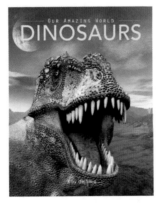

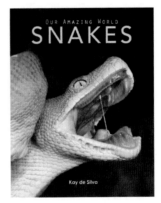

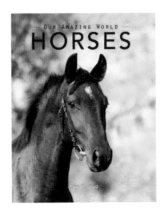

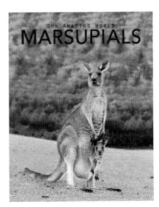

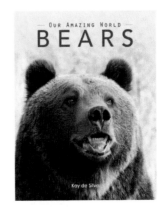

Aurora
An imprint of CKTY Publishing Solutions

www.ouramazingworldbooks.com

Made in the USA
Lexington, KY
12 January 2017